MILLION DOLLAR LOVE LETTERS

MILLION DOLLAR LOVE LETTERS

Words from the heart of a wise, old soul

JOE SPEARS

iUniverse, Inc.
Bloomington

MILLION DOLLAR LOVE LETTERS

iUniverse books may be ordered through booksellers or by contacting:

iUniverse
1663 Liberty Drive
Bloomington, IN 47403
www.iuniverse.com
1-800-Authors (1-800-288-4677)

ISBN: 978-1-4620-5492-3 (sc)
ISBN: 978-1-4620-5493-0 (e)

Library of Congress Control Number: 2011916474

Printed in the United States of America

iUniverse rev. date: 10/4/2011

Dedication

To the one I love...thank you.

A special thanks to:

Photographer: David Gaertner
Friends and Editors: Susan Panzarella
and Gretchen Gaertner
Editorial staff at iUniverse
My family and friends who have
inspired me

New Love

Chapter One

Why Do I Love You?

Why do I love you?
You are the air I breathe
And the breath I take.
You are my life, my love, my all.
Your love binds my spirit, and
Truer love I have never known—
Heart to heart, body and soul.
Your smile could heal a broken heart.
My world and love are wrapped in your arms
And I take each challenge in life
With courage and confidence.
We voyage through life, letting our souls
Decide our destiny.
Only with wisdom comes joy,
And with greatness, a love like yours.
I wish you dreams that light your mind.
Togetherness is the spiritual food
That feeds my hungry soul.
Join me on the journey to Eternity.
Deeply you marked me in passion.
Kindly my senses accept your love;
Its intensity has become my treasure.
You soothe my restlessness
And banish the thoughts of day.
Your kiss good-night inspires my heart
And shapes my tomorrow.
May you have someone to greet you,
Adventures to meet you,
And my love to keep you.

My darling,

It was once said of the man who discovered the North Pole,

"Let no one come and talk about luck and chance;

It is the strong man who looks ahead."

You came into my life like a gift from heaven

And soon slipped into my heart's treasury.

Let us forget the storms of yesterday,

And all the cold, blustery winter days.

But remember the flowers that bloom

And the birds that sing and God,

Who studies each soul.

With every dew drop as a thought from God's soul,

Dearest, you make me a better person, just knowing you care.

It takes many hands to do the work of God.

My darling,
What is loving you like?
It's like sitting in my kitchen,
Watching the birds enjoy the loaf of bread I just gave them.
They were in the trees, waiting for me to feed them.
They waited patiently,
The way I hunger for your smile, your embrace,
The touch of your moist lips,
That's what loving you is like.
You can never do too much for the one you love.
I miss you when you are out of sight.
I miss you more while alone
When there's a full moon or a dark night.
Hurry back to me.

Good morning, my goddess,

A life without you and your love would be no life at all.

Paradise was made for tender hearts such as yours and mine, honey.

It is not difficult to know at what moment life began with you.

When our eyes met, I knew I wanted you in my life forever.

I love you for everything you've done

To make our life together a happy one.

You are my love. Can I say that too much?

For I will never stop feeling this way.

Dearest,

What is love?

Setting goals for the future with the one you love.

Staying focused and ready to help anyone.

Following a plan but having flexibility for change,

Giving thanks when needed.

May all we share together in the future

Be the beginning of the best years of our lives.

So much comfort, so much care.

Love shared is a celebration of life in itself.

Two hearts together, sharing the true love of the other,

The memory of happy days spent together

With the promise of new joys ahead.

May this be the start of a new life for you and me.

I will try harder to carry my load.

I love you so much.

Thank you for the time you give me.

My dearest love,
I have never loved the way I love you.
Whatever we do, wherever we go,
You are like a great queen.
We are not drawn from behind but lured from before,
Never pushed but pulled, magnetized from beyond,
Like a love that lasts forever
Or a never-ending friendship.
Like the courage you give me that I can trust in
And know in my heart that it's never failing.
An unworthy thought obscures joyous, radiant living,
My eyes see your beauty, and life continues onward flowing.
May all my love, courage, faith, and affection
Make your life as complete as you have made mine.

My darling,
I want to love you with all I have,
Live well and laugh often together.
Let us be worthy of each other,
Showing the respect we deserve.
One commandment is to love one another.
When a man loves his woman,
She in turn will respect her man
And be equal with him as one in the sight of God.
Together we can accomplish the desire God has for our lives.
We can make it! And it's going to be glorious!

Dear,

As you walk, opening a new door of life, I follow.
Closing the door behind you and never looking back.
I only look forward to seeing what new adventure
Is on the other side of the wishing well!
The last months I've spent with you in my life
Have brought joy, laughter, and love to my heart;
True moments of caring and days of sharing
With a love I thought I would never experience.
You make life bright and new!
So this day, I promise to love you
With a love that's true and never take you for granted.
I will take adequate time to listen and show you I care,
With a special love that grows strong and deeper as time goes by.
I'll be gentle and kind with your hopes, joys, tears, and cares.
All my love I send to you in this letter, today and always.

Dear,

I hear a whisper of love blowing your way,

Blowing my love to your soft, sweet lips,

Blowing the love of my heart to yours.

Once again, I give you my life,

For without you there is no life.

I offer you this declaration of love.

The world is only an open space unless you are in it.

I feel I was born to be by your side.

I never lack words when I write.

I just think how I hunger for your touch.

My tongue confesses my love for you

As my body grows so lonely for yours.

How I miss the moistness of your passionate lips!

I crave all of you,

Every inch of your body, with my heart bubbling over,

Concerned only for your desires.

Sometimes I feel ridiculous

Writing all the things I do.

Maybe it's foolish.

If so, please forgive me and destroy all these letters.

They just seem to be the only way

To express the true feelings I hold inside my heart

And the genuine love I feel for you.

From the first time my eyes looked upon your beauty and we met,

I truly fell in love with you.

And my life has changed only for the better since then.

My dearest love,
Such a sense of loss when you're not with me!
How you engulf me at times with your actions
And enhance my life with your beauty!
For all this, I give you my personal admiration
Plus all the warmth and love I feel for you.
Just being away from you this evening is punishment enough!
A feeling of repentance comes over me.
Yes, dear, I love you truly and deeply,
Never less, but always more.
Please, do not doubt my love for you!
When with you, I feel your trust, your strength,
And most of all, your love.
How wonderful I feel when you're in my arms.
I don't want just to try to be clever with you,
But to touch your heart and soul.

My love,

Today is my birthday, my first birthday with you.

I ask myself this question:

If it were your birthday instead of mine,

And I were home sick,

Would you go dancing this evening without me?

Definitely not!

If I honestly believed that you would,

Then the last months that we've been together were wasted,

And the lady I fell in love with never even existed.

In short, I would rather spend five minutes on the phone with you

Than an evening on the dance floor

Holding another woman in my arms, wishing she were you.

Pick out what you want to watch on television,

And I'll watch the same program.

Just another way we can be together in spirit,

Just another way to say, "Yes, I love you more than words can say."

Your beauty has completely captured my soul.

My love for you is precious and eternal.

I feel my heartbeat when I look upon your beauty

And realize I love nothing more on this earth

Than the way you have touched my soul

With your charm and affectionate ways.

You share precious moments of passion, love, and quality.

You give me your all.

I feel so wonderful about the bond the two of us share.

I never knew such love as this existed in this world.

I pray it will go into the next!

I know I want only to share my life and love with you.

You have stirred a passion within me that didn't know I had.

When I hold you in my arms on the dance floor,

I feel the blood rushing to my heart.

Tell me I'm not dreaming!

My dearest,

As I watched the movie *Love Is a Many-Splendored Thing*,

I thought of you and me.

The actor William Holden said,

"Many mistakes are made in the name of loneliness."

I thought of you and me.

I don't want us to be a mistake!

I want our love to be soft, gentle, and kind;

Ordained by God.

To you, I want to be as good as the happiness

And pleasure you bring to me.

I want to be the strength

And yet the tenderness you need in your life.

I want us to come alive together

And grow even more in love in the future.

Every day we are not together is a day gone forever.

Yes, darling, I love you with all my heart.

Dearest,

Your girlfriends are precious,

And I can see that you mean the world to them.

I want to thank you for all the time

You set aside in your busy life for me.

You are such a quality lady!

I know you choose your friends carefully,

And I respect the loyalty you have for other people.

Each hour I spend with you is time I spend in paradise!

A reunion we all search for.

Each week that passes, I feel closer to you.

Some nights when I go to bed,

I miss having you by my side

And feeling your warm body next to me.

How proud I feel when you walk with me!

How I treasure the pleasant moments we spend together!

I'm looking forward to this evening.

Spending time with you and family is always a joy to me!

Dearest,

What a special evening last night!

You are more precious than gold

And so very delightful to be with.

How alone I was until you came into my life.

Thank you for your prayers and support.

I know this has been the most difficult time of the year,

Yet you've spent extra time with me.

You've been that wonderful bright spot in my life.

And your family, with all their kindness,

Has been an unspeakable blessing.

No wonder! They have *you*!

I will always carry special thoughts and prayers in my heart

Just for you and your exceptional family.

I hope this Christmas turns out to be the way you wished it to be.

Because of you, this has been for me

One of the warmest and happiest seasons, filled with joy and love.

And I know it will be followed

By a bright New Year because of you.

I wonder if I could love you even more if you were my wife!

Perhaps a little!

I will never have a complete Christmas without you in it,

For the greatest, best gift in my life has been you and your love!

You are so worthy of praise.

Just your presence thrills my heart and soul.

I'm touched deep within by every breath you take,

My dearest sweetheart.

My love,

Is this true love we feel and share?

When we are apart, I feel lonely;

So I close my eyes and think

How wonderful it is when you're in my arms.

I hear you say, "Dear, what are you thinking this moment?"

And I see those beautiful eyes of yours

Cutting deep into my soul.

At that very second, I want my lips touching your lips,

Your cheeks, your eyes, your ears, your neck, your body.

You are close even when you are away,

For I keep you within my heart.

When you get lonely,

Just reach out and I will feel your gentle touch.

Yes, you are that friend who I love.

It was meant to be.

When I first met you, I knew in my heart

That a lasting friendship—and more—was beginning.

How fortunate I am to have you in my life.

My dearest,

Thank you for last evening, a meal fit for a king!

What is a king without his queen, dining and dancing?

I ask myself what I have done to deserve such happiness.

I think back to the trip we took to the beach.

If you had had that extra glass of wine,

I can only imagine the love we would have made together!

Could I have made it through the night?

But you were so strong in your resolve.

I have to admit, I admire you for that quality.

You just wait, and I will also,

Until God has joined us together as one at the altar.

That will be a monumental day for Love.

Dearest,

I have never felt closer to you than I did last evening!

I just wanted to take you home with me and make love to you.

That would have made it a perfect weekend!

You shared a lot of your personal life with me,

And I appreciate that so very much.

When I held you close to me,

I knew I wanted you in my life forever,

Not just for your body, but for your eyes,

Your smile, your funny, soft laugh, your humor,

The way you move when you get serious about something,

The way you hold my hand at the movies or when I pray,

And your precious kindness to my family and me.

I want you to know I've waited all my life to meet, love, and

Share myself with another person, like you.

And with your help, we can have a good life,

A good time, happy moments, and not a lot of sadness.

We can welcome with open arms each day

That morning brings sunshine into our lives

And if you will allow me,

I would like to embrace you.

My arms are wide open!

And share those mornings of sunshine

With the greatest lady I have ever known—*you*!

Daily I pray this: Give me the strength, dear Lord,

To raise my mind high above all daily trifles

And to surrender my strength to your will with my love.

Let me know the meaning of your heart

And, better yet, understand it.

Dearest,

What a pleasure talking to you last evening!
The more I talk to you,
The more I appreciate all the good qualities I see.
I love the way we are together!
I've known you for a while now,
But I know so little about you;
Yet you know too much about me!
I miss being with you, feeling your love.
Is that asking so much?
Maybe just a little.
But I miss your laugh, your smile,
Your wit when I'm not with you.
And nothing can replace your beauty and charm.
Your tender love is like a warm melody
Playing a tune of its own for you and me.
We need to share the sound of beautiful music together
Or make some of our own!
When I hold you in my arms,
For whatever reason, it feels right.
You make everything complete.
I'm so glad you are in my life.

My dearest,

I missed being with you this evening.

You have brought so much happiness into my life

In such a short time!

You are the most astonishing and amazing person I have ever met!

With you, I would never go astray;

I trust your judgment and your ability to make the right choices in life.

You have the charisma of a queen,

A gift of God's grace,

A quality of leadership that has captured my imagination.

You have a special charm about you that I have come to love.

What a world of happiness I have found with you!

I hope I don't bore you too much with my simple words, sweetheart.

You are the woman I thought I would never meet,

And here I am, head-over-heels in love with you!

My love,
How beautiful you were last evening!
How precious, how fair!
A sweet smile, words soft-spoken
With tenderness and watchfulness and care.
The moistened eye, the firmness of your lips,
Now and then a simple sigh,
Never an expression of doubt or fear.
You were my gentle, kind, trusting, and loving playmate.
May our hearts, our hopes, our prayers, our tears,
And our faith triumph over any of life's difficulties
And be bathed in celestial light—
Like the glory and the freshness of a beautiful dream
On a bright and sunny June day.
Though I leave you for a while,
Only the words are gone.
I will stay with you forever.

My midnight star,
You shine like a rose in the early morning dew.
Never does a day or an hour go by
That thoughts of you are not on my mind.
You are where pity ends and love begins.
You are the best part of my life!
You make everything beautiful,
With meaning, difference, and purpose.
I feel young and alive when I'm with you.
There are so many places I want to take you.
I pray God will give us a little more time
So that we can travel the world over together.
I want our love to last forever.
As long as we are together,
My heart will know no greater happiness.

Dearest darling,

How lucky I am to have you in my life!

I love you more than my dearest possessions.

I want to spend the rest of my life with you.

All I can give you is my love, understanding, and kindness,

But you deserve a lot more.

I was just admiring the beautiful flowers you gave me.

I have them near the fireplace

So that when I sit in front of it,

I can see them and your picture on the mantel at the same time.

Thank you for the call this morning.

You seemed better.

How I've missed you these last few days.

Stay well.

My darling,
A thousand apologies I offer you
To express any wrong I have ever caused you in any way,
For I hold you dearest in my heart.
I find an attraction in you that so draws me in.
You are so appealing, attractive, and interesting
That you arouse a very favorable response from me.
I want to hold you and love you.
I want to put lotion on your hands
And rub it in until there's no more,
Then on your feet, your beautiful legs, your back,
The front of you—the whole time kissing you
And speaking with soft words, almost a whisper,
"My darling, you are the love of my life!"
When we are together,
Let me hold you close and embrace you.
I love your meaningful kisses.
How I long to see you this moment.

My dearest,
How do you feel when you fall in love?
Can I speak for myself?
It's a pleasure to be alive,
Just to get up in the morning,
My heart jumps just thinking of you.
I wash my face, I think of you.
I comb my hair, I think of your beautiful hair.
When we dance, you touch my hair;
Then you pull away
As though you committed an offensive crime.
If you only knew how much I love
To feel your wonderful touch on my body.
It only makes our love stronger.
So fast the world goes by!
Let us succeed and give
If it helps you live.
Darling, I have loved you for a long time now,
The best time of my life.
How perfect it would be if you would be my loving wife!

My precious,
The more time I spend with you,
The more I care for you.
The more I love you,
The more I want and need you.
You, my love, will be mine
And I will be yours till the end of time.
What have I found and discovered in you that I needed?
Strength and fortitude, courage,
The ability to take what life gives me and press forward.
For once, I know why God has kept me alive!
If it was only to be with you for this short time
It has been worth the pleasure you have given me.
Just to look into my eyes
And see your pleasant smile makes my heart
Continue to beat within me.
You have given me spiritual wisdom and faith,
Devotion with sacrificial love.
You have given me *you*!
For this I am eternally grateful.

To the One I Love

Chapter Two

You Take My Breath Away

You take my breath away
When I gaze upon your beauty.
You take my breath away
When I look into your eyes.
You take my breath away
When I see you smile.
You take my breath away
When I kiss you with such pleasure.
You take my breath away
When I hold you tight
In the quiet of the darkness.
You take my breath away
When you lay by my side.
Now I know you have captured my soul.
How I fancy the coming morning
Knowing soon the sunlight
Will meet the morning sky.
May the hours of our passion
Be brought to the morning of perfect bliss.
Hurt froze my heart, but your love melted it.
My dearest love, you take my breath away.

My dearest love,
If at any time the road seems a little lonely,
Slow down and let me walk by your side.
Let me be your support and comfort.
If you want to talk, I will be there to listen.
I enjoyed your company so much Thursday morning.
Fantastic breakfast and your beautiful smile,
A kiss so sweet, plus a hug and caress.
When your bravery wears down and you want to be alone,
No problem; maybe a quiet time to meditate
Or cry, if you like, would be just what you need.
If you want anything,
Without hesitation, give me a call.
At times we need space, time alone,
I'll try never to smother you.
I want you to know that you are most precious to me.
My love never changes, no matter what.
My prayers are with you until all of your pain goes away.
God's prayer is that God's will be done.
Deeper faith will increase courage and blessings.
Let us believe His word and promise.
I close this letter with a warm, heartfelt prayer,
Sent to heaven, asking the Lord to bless you with good health,
Forever with Him.
It's such a short time ....

Dearest,

Let us lie together in the still of bliss as the darkness becomes light.

I can see the sunshine on your face.

When the days are numbered and the hours short,

We will play hard and rest longer.

As we fade into the light of the coming day,

As we inherit the human element of sweet purity,

Where music is life and gladness is night,

Place your hand inside mine, oh beautiful lady,

And be my love this night.

How can I forget the sweetness of your eyes smmiling with the mystery of life?

Just the thought thrills my heart with boundless you

And lasting memories.

The great Socrates said in the last hour of life,

"Be of good cheer, and bury my body only."

And they did!

A saying of Plato's was,

"He is not dead; he has just gone away!"

Oh spotless woman in the world of shame,

Full of splendor and silent scorn,

Go back to God while you can.

You are the kindest warrior in the land!

As this day ends and your love begins,

It's never what you say but only what you are.

Dearest love,

Happy anniversary!

I hope the stars and moon that shine on you tonight

Remind you of that special one … me.

I wish we were in the moonlight together.

The joys of you are heaven on earth.

Next time we meet, we will make up for this absence.

If I were there, I would take you dancing and celebrate.

Here's wishing you sweet music, sweet memories,

And the love I hold in my heart.

Don't forget me, your favorite playmate!

Dear,

Don't just count the months we celebrate!

Count the good times we've shared,

Count the stars we've wished on,

Count all the lovely memories

And then add a thousand

Just for each time we've been together.

Fill each moment with delight.

My prayer is this:

Gracious Lord, hold my lady friend close to your heart. Grant her a speedy recovery, good health, and a strong heart, for she is that special someone in my life.

Dearest,

How the time has flown since I first met you!
I can't believe we've been together for over a year.
I will never forget the way you looked the night I met you,
The memories we have shared since then,
And the pure joy you have brought into my life.
Now and then I have asked God what I have done
To deserve someone as nice as you,
And then I just thank Him!
I shall unveil my thoughts to you.
Listen carefully, my dearest love,
Hear my heart cry out for your sweet kiss.
Must I plead so?
My soul I give freely as a hidden scent in a rose.
Your passion is so soft and quiet,
"Why do you sigh this night?"
I whispered low; and you replied,
"I think I'm in your heart tonight."
Lie by me throughout the night
With your love and tender grace.
Let me take you tonight,
Or let me live alone in my security.
Will you fill my room with your love this night,
Oh lady from heaven, with open eyes?
As I lie beside you, with open eyes?
As I lie beside you with my soul aching so,
I know that my life without you would only be
Like the wind blowing the tides,
Yet I yearn for the fulfillment our intimacy would bring.

Dearest,

I need to write you a little more after the last letter.

With you, the word *together* warms my soul.

A lot of my friends are gone away and no longer available.

Let us not weep, my love, for wild thoughts of the past.

That time is gone, so let it be.

I can hear those words from your sweet lips.

Let us sing to our old friends,

Though their days have hurried by,

And we think warm days will never cease,

But soon we die. Of course, me first,

My lovely one, being the older of the two of us!

I just heard in my heart a sweet, sweet voice—yours!

A voice from heaven.

You are my angel, my queen, and my dearest love.

My love, my sweet,

Just the thought of you warms my heart.

Yet in my heart of hearts,

I feel your strength, your might;

The true calling of a Christian is not to do extraordinary things,

But to do ordinary things in an extraordinary way!

You do that!

True joy comes not to him who seeks it for himself,

But to him who seeks it for others.

No one knows this better than you!

My love,

These are words spoken from my unconquerable zone,

Beyond the place of wrath and tears,

Unafraid as I walk straight, facing all punishment,

Hopefully, as a master of my fate or a captain of my soul.

Yes, my darling, forever and a day,

Never will I stray;

And I shall keep you in the depths of my soul.

Let the rains come and the floodwaters rise,

For with you by my side, I fear nothing.

So as we go forth into the beyond,

Let there be nothing more valued than kindness,

Nothing more sacred than honor,

And nothing so loyal or more precious as your love for me.

My true love,

What, really, are you to me?

If I were asked this question by someone else,

What would be my answer (from my heart)?

I will tell you first that I admit

I was lonely for the right companion

For many, many years.

When you came along,

I had a feeling there was something very special about you.

When you hugged me to comfort me one evening,

It was more of a consoling hug than anything romantic.

But I felt something,

The something I hadn't felt but had missed having in my life.

You have turned out to be

The one person in my life with whom I can dare to be myself.

You are a true friend, a playmate, a buddy and pal.

You're a friend to chide me when I'm wrong

Or allow me to share my innermost soul.

And that friendship has proved to be

As strong for you as it has been for me.

I thank you for coming by last evening.

It meant a lot to me.

A few moments of bliss,

A little romantic music,

A couple of dances—

All of these things make the week seem short

And life a little brighter.

And somehow the loneliness just disappears.

When you cancel other events and make room for me in your life,

I am truly honored and touched

By your willingness to share your kindness,

Your love, your generosity, yourself.

I love you because
You have done more than anyone could have done
To make me happy—
By just being yourself!

Good morning, princess,

How tender are the moments we share?

As I look into your eyes,

I feel the love burning with passion in the depths of my soul,

A love that is sent from your heart.

It is a love that is overdue,

That can only be accepted by another waiting heart

As the two of us become one.

Let us give life to our faith and to our destiny.

I want only what is best for you,

I want your future to be as bright, sweet, and tender

As your loving and caring smile.

You possess enough compassion in your heart to rule a kingdom.

You will always be my queen.

From the moment we met, I knew my destiny would change.

So lovely to look at,

You are like the touch of sunlight

Or the soft morning air blowing,

Or a precious sweet kiss when I say good night.

You are the rose I hold dear to my heart.

I believe we can get what we want in life,

If we are willing to pay the price

And want it bad enough.

Nothing in life is as good as two minds working as one.

And you, my dear,

Are what I want!

Dearest,

Nothing could make life more precious

Than having you by my side.

Just your smile warms my heart.

When I think of you and all the blessings you've brought into my life,

Words seem too little to give you in return.

You are a great example and an inspiration,

Always touching the hearts of whomever you meet.

So today I send a special greeting.

The thought of all the love you've given me is so wonderful.

The joy has touched my heart and filled my soul.

Your beauty I see while watching the sunset's golden hue.

A love like this cannot be measured in gold or silver

Or by a few simple words,

But by sharing time together.

I'm so thankful that you came into my life.

The longer we are together

And the more I know about you,

The more I respect you and your wishes.

It's all the little things you do—

Gifts given from your heart, a cheerful smile,

Now and then a special word,

A thoughtful look, a sympathetic nod,

Or the way you run your fingers though your hair.

These are just a few of the gifts I treasure.

And then there's the sexy way you move across the room

Without even meaning to!

Love like this cannot be bought,

Only given from the heart.

Thank you for all the beautiful times we've had.

My darling,

My life and my soul are always soothed by your presence,

My heart, filled with joy and tenderness,

With a sweet sentiment.

I worship and live for you.

From one lovely week to the next,

Some days my heart aches with the loneliness

I feel from missing you so.

Soon you will arrive.

Your beauty is breathtaking,

And my heart is touched by your kind words and generous behavior.

You came into my life like a soft breeze,

Filling my heart with all your charm, beauty, and love,

Saying these words:

"I am the wind, your life, your love.

Just close your eyes and know you are in heaven."

Dearest,

I just hung up from talking to you on the phone.

It was so nice hearing your voice in the morning.

One week from today is Mother's Day.

I know you're not my mother,

But I do know how precious you are.

So let me pass on a little extra special love

I hold in my heart for all mothers!

I thought God had given me everything in life I needed to be happy,

And then He gave me you!

When I think of you,

I know what real happiness is all about.

Then I know how blessed I am.

Thank you for coming into my life.

You are truly the greatest lady I know.

Even when the words go unspoken,

The love for you is still in my heart.

I say all this just to let you know how much you are loved.

Happy Mother's Day, a little early!

My darling,

I feel your strength when you walk by my side.

I feel your love when I look into your eyes,

A love that is true and honest.

I could never hold another woman in my arms

Now that I've held you.

My beautiful one,

You have only to smile to bring true color into life.

That is the way you are!

Your tenderness can change total darkness to light.

I can close my eyes and see you and me,

Walking on the beach,

Feeling the sand on our feet,

Kissing like we were young once again.

A clean life full of fun, knowing no wrong,

Full of romance, love, and charm,

Feeling young again.

I stop to pray a small prayer

To thank God for bringing you into my life.

My dearest,

Elizabeth Barrett Browning wrote,

"How do I love thee? Let me count the ways."

I will let my heart speak the words—

The words are too precious for lips to utter.

You are my angel of mercy.

Every breath I take is a gamble

That I can look upon your beauty another day.

Then I feel like the lord of the world!

Your love has come quietly and softly,

Like a drop of water cutting though a rock.

Your love for me is the water,

And my heart is the rock.

Freely I tell you this.

I could not love you more if you were my wife.

You are the finest, most dedicated person I know.

For all you are, I love you.

For who you are, I love you still.

My dearest,

Let me put a few words to my feelings!

Daniel Webster said it well:

"Without the Bible, man would be in the midst of a sandy desert;

Surrounded on all sides by a dark and impenetrable horizon."

I would add that salvation is not by our works

But by the grace of God.

We are not saved because we are earnest;

But he who is not earnest

Has an earnest reason to question

Whether or not he is really saved.

The one who lives well can preach well.

Maybe that's another priority we need to understand.

And finally, a person who speaks truth

And loves it must be reckoned precious by any human society.

Thank you for allowing me to bare my soul.

Dearest,

What a great lady!

You have honor and self-respect,

And the wisdom to embrace these qualities in all you do.

Life is a series of surprises

And would not be worth living

If it were not so.

Why do I love you?

I am certain we were brought together

For more of a reason than to be lovers.

We are soul mates

With the bonus of love that is the sweetness of flowers.

I had such a wonderful time with you over the weekend;

I must admit, I didn't want it to end.

I watch you during the time I'm with you

And learn more about you:

The way you understand things,

The way you think,

The good judgment you show,

The common sense you bring to each situation.

I do so admire your sincerity and the heartfelt way

You share yourself with everyone who is close to you.

I love you more each day!

And with everyone you meet,

You leave just a little of yourself.

So, humbly I thank you for sharing and giving me

A little piece of your precious heart!

Let me feel the lovability of every soul

I meet along the way, as you do.

My prayer is this:

May my love for you be perfect with a true spirit clothed in mortal clay,

with a nearness that is perilous and sweet.

The Family
We Choose

Chapter Three

My Angel

Thank you for the kind gift!
I'll accept that for Father's Day.
That way, I'll feel a lot younger!
I love holding your hand,
Seeing you smile,
Kissing you, dancing with you,
Even sharing a sip of water with you.
My sweet, you, and you alone
Make my dreams come true.
You are so easy to love,
So easy to talk to, so easy to be myself around
And share my thoughts with.
My burning passion
Is to bring you close to my heart.
With you, I have reached deep inside my soul
To understand myself,
To know what true love really means—
Not just to me but to you, also.
And I know that I truly love you.
You are so wonderful to me.
You are like springtime
When snow is on the ground.
I am touched by your tenderness and charm.
I had a serious talk with the Lord about you.
He agreed that you are special
And the perfect mate for me.
So I'll be patient and wait
For you to realize the same fact!
Meanwhile,
I'll enjoy loving you.

My Sweet Sick Baby

All my thoughts and prayers are that you'll get well.
I feel your pain and love,
Adore, desire, and worship only you!
I want to hold you and no other.
Your loving words lift me out of this world into the next.
God spoke to me the words,
And I saw the light.
Let the words sink into your heart,
Lift you up as they penetrate your soul,
Teaching every fiber of your being,
Knowing the universe isn't large enough
To contain all the love my heart holds
For you, my dearest.
As I continue, I am overpowered by the love
I want to share with you.
Oh, how heavy my heart beats,
Knowing you are not feeling well,
Being away from you when you might need help.
The longing is deep.
This precious love I feel,
A love of our unity,
Bonding us together, forever and always.
My heart is touched by these simple
But humble and kind words.
You are my new beginning,
My new passion in life.
I hunger to protect you,
And I promise to love you
Desperately, with all my heart, forever.

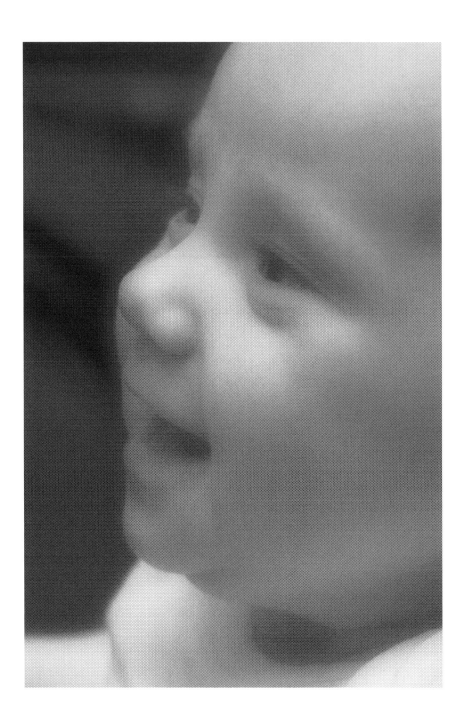

Little Girl of Mine

Little girl of mine,
My dearest daughter,
It seems just yesterday that you were a child.
When you were born, the angels started singing.
And when God looked down to earth and saw you,
How he smiled!
He knew already then that you were special.
I found that out much more slowly.
And today, as with all the days before,
I feel blessed that he entrusted you to your mother and me.
How did I doubt that when this day arrived
You'd be standing beside the perfect mate,
A gentle man who loves and understands you,
A partner picked by God, not fate?
Your mother and I watched you join hands,
Recite your vows with hope and tears.
And God's presence, just as always,
Is blessing you from above.
You carried each other's joy through life,
And along with the joys, there have come sorrows.
So this is the cross you've accepted with love
From that day on and for all your tomorrows.
It is with love this poem is written for you both,
And with love it is shared with you today
With hope for a long and joyous marriage.

My Wonderful Daughter

In your sweet and thoughtful ways, you are the source of all my pride. Your smile reflects the true beauty you got from your precious mother, as well as a warm, caring spirit and heart of gold. You share all of the joys life can hold.

Kim, I am so proud of you. No matter what you do, I know it will be right. Your love always comes shining through; and of all the joys of living, the best is having a kind, caring daughter like you. In the years past, you have been a friend and someone to be proud of and appreciate. You mean the world to me.

Your birthday tells a story of how beautiful life can be when it holds so much warmth, friendship, and love. Who wouldn't love someone as wonderful as you?

May happiness be at the heart of everything you do. May joy be your best friend, and any worries fall at your footsteps. May your dreams wait patiently while you catch up. Therefore, on your birthday, and from that day forward, may you know how much you are loved by your devoted husband, your precious children, Cort and Tyler, and your many caring friends.

All my love I give to a daughter who grows more special every year.

Happy birthday!

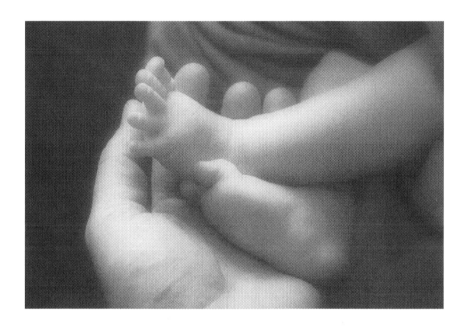

Gift From Heaven

September 15, 2010
Little girl of ours, our dearest daughter, Mary Elizabeth,
It seems just yesterday that you were born.
The angels started singing, and God looked down to earth and he smiled.
He knew already that you were special.
And today, as with all the days before,
We feel blessed that the Lord entrusted you to me and your mother,
Elizabeth. The precious name Mary,
Is also the name of the mother of our Lord Jesus.
Mary Elizabeth in Hebrew means "God is my oath."
In English literature, there are seven names taken from your beautiful
name Elizabeth: Bess, Bessie, Beth, Betsy, Elise, Lisa, and Liz.
Mary Elizabeth.
Your name was first used in the year 1533
By a great lady named Elizabeth Petrovna.
Many years later, King Henry VIII and his wife, Ann Boleyn,
Had a daughter, and they named her Elizabeth after this lady.
John the Baptist's mother's name was also Elizabeth.
A great English poet, Elizabeth Barrett Browning,
Wrote a beautiful poem to her husband, Robert.
It begins … "How do I love thee? Let me count the ways."
Mary Elizabeth,
Time will pass us by,
But heartfelt memories will last forever.
Mary Elizabeth,
You will be a great lady like your mother, Elizabeth, and her mother.
You will walk with pride, charm, and grace.
You will have the courage and faith to stand tall and walk proud.
You will have wisdom, strength, and love in your heart.
May God always bless you and your family.

My Soul Mate—
Jim & Becky

Jim truly is the gem you see.
Jim loves to work and loves to play,
Living life to the fullest.
One lucky lady I am.
Jim's soul is a stake to be won.
I surrender my strength, my heart,
And all my love to Jim, my soul mate.
He is known for his courage and knowledge.
Jim is as good as goodness gets.
One day at work I got a call from Jim.
I was so excited!
My heart pounding, I said,
"My darling Jim, it is you!"
Such a kind and caring voice,
Jim, my soul mate.
Whenever I awaken during the night for any reason,
I feel for his human touch.
With a sigh of relief,
I feel safe and secure, once again,
In the arms of Jim, my soul mate!

J.A.M.

Jeanette, Ann, and Marilyn:
Mr. Webster would say,
"A thick mixture of preserves."
Joe says,
"A mixture of love that God sent from heaven
And placed in three separate hearts of women destined to meet
And share a lifetime bond of real friendship."
These ladies were willing to go through stormy weather together,
Thus giving true meaning to the word *friendship*.
Yes, you are "jammed" together,
with a love that is the essence of your souls.
There will be change,
But you will never lose the spirit of your friendship.
Love is in knowing that each of you can be alone,
But none of you will be lonely,
For you will always know
The other two are there for you.
This bond you have is exemplified
When you gather Friday afternoons at the Charlotte Café.
What you each give is essential to the joy of your frienship.
When J.A.M. gets together,
There's a powerful force:
A force like this may change the universe!

Art and His Soul Mate, Brenda

When I say something to you, Art, and you're touched by it,
You kiss me on the cheek!
...You really have me talking to myself.
What do I have here?
Is this another *Brokeback Mountain* with two cowboys?
Who just love "ridin', ropin', and redecoratin'."
Just for the record, I'm too short to be a cowboy
And I would need a stepladder to get on a horse.
As it turns out, Art, you like to kiss everyone,
Especially your cowgirl and soul mate, Brenda.
Life is great when you find the right soul mate.
The little lady may have started out as your playmate,
And then you realized you had found the love of your life.
She has that special smile and sweet voice that melted your heart.
You love Brenda enough to understand her needs and wants,
Likes and dislikes.
You share a closeness with her that stirs the immortality of your soul.
When you're lucky enough to find this love,
Don't question it; accept it.
Some things in life are meant to be;
Yes, you are one of the lucky ones!
You have found your soul mate to share your destiny.
Celebrate each moment that you experience together.
I speak for everyone when I say,
We all love you and wish you the best life has to offer.

Cort and Mr. T

These next few years will shape your lives.
What little advice can I offer you
That may help in some small way?
I see in the future romance and love for both of you,
Just around the corner!
As a grandfather, I couldn't be prouder.
You both have grown into perfect gentlemen.
You are like a breath of heaven
With million dollar smiles for all who know you.
The family and I appreciate the way
You each guard and protect your reputation,
For it's one of your most valuable assets.
Neither of you has ever known self-pity,
Which shows strength of character.
Your performance in life will only improve with age,
Like a fine wine.
Both of you have the wisdom, good understanding,
The right attitude, and love in your hearts to be winners.
Here are a few pearls my father, your great-grandfather,
Passed on to me, always saying to my brother and me,
"Men, remember this,"
And then the words of wisdom would come pouring out!
I think they still hold true today:
First impressions are most important, especially with a young lady!
If you always have to be right, no matter what,
You'll find yourselves having to apologize often for being wrong!
Remember, true love comes from the heart, with deep passion.
Be a friend to all and you will always have friends.
You can do all things in life if you have the faith.
Think like a millionaire and you will live like one.

Stay away from people who only want to use you.

Always follow your gut feeling. That is your inner soul telling you what to do.

Listen to your brother, Mr. T! He loves you and will never tell you wrong.

Good luck, my men!

My City

You are a breathtaking city!
In the springtime, approximately ten years ago,
I visited here for the first time
And fell in love with you.
In my travels around the country,
No other place measures up to your happy wonder,
With the goodness of nature and the blessings of God!
You have a beauty that touches the heavens.
You are like the great queen for whom you were named.
Two years ago, I flew back from Indiana
To see if you were as fantastic as I remembered.
I found you to be even more so!
In fact, I was so taken by your beauty
That I made a few important calls;
And without even leaving here, in the blink of an eye,
I was now in my new home.
You've brought something special into my life
With your terrific weather,
The closeness of the wondrous mountains,
And your incredible sunrises and sunsets.
You have captured my soul,
And there's no looking back!
Were I to leave you, the longing memories
Would haunt me until I returned.
Your abundant trees, waterfalls, and lovely flowers
Would call out to me, to the far reaches of the earth.
Oh, what joy, laughter, and true happiness you have added to my life!
How good is this warm feeling called
home.

Maria

Maria Theresa, my darling wife:
This letter celebrates your next birthday,
Our anniversary, and Christmas.
It share with you how precious,
Loving, and charming you are.
Maria, I love your name,
A name of European nobility.
When I speak it, music starts playing.
"Maria, Maria, Maria," a lovely symphony.
What a kind and beautiful wife you are;
I adore, honor and idolize you.
I worship and treasure your sweet kisses.
Maria, you are my life and my dearest love.
When I think of you, I feel your embrace
And your soft touch.
The sweetness of your love blinds my vision.
My love Maria, your gentle ways
Brings me the strength that I need,
With the essence of love.
My love for you has no end.
Your faith is radiant and strong,
And your beauty is everlasting.
You are the joy that makes my life complete.
I never knew what a king felt like
Until you became my queen.
Before I met you, heaven seemed so far away.
With you by my side,
The journey is as sweet as the destination.

Elsie

Elsie was my buddy.
I never thought of Elsie
Without remembering John.
The world was their dance floor.
Each partner loved and respected the other
Completely and unconditionally,
Always moving together as one.
For them, life was playing the music
To their own tune and rhythm,
With two hearts beating as one.
As the years quickly passed by,
Their love for each other only grew stronger.
This is the true essence of human love.
John, this is when Elsie would ask you
To walk with faith and hope in your heart,
Behind the silence of every new day.
Elsie is gone in body,
But in spirit she will never be more
Than a step away from the love of her life, John.
Elsie touched the hearts
Of everyone who crossed her path.
May we all find comfort
In the memory of her love.
To a gracious lady like Elsie,
You never say good-bye;
Instead, say, "We loved you while you were here on Earth
And just the same now that you are in heaven."
Last night I talked to Elsie.
I asked for her permission
For a moment of silent prayer to celebrate,
A few days early their fifty-seventh wedding anniversary.

Kindly with a smile she replied,
"Joe, if it is okay with John.
Just don't make a mess in the kitchen
Or dent the car."
Now let's take a moment of silence for John and Elsie.

Opal

Opal really was her first name
In more than one way.
Her parents surely saw her
As their newborn jewel.
Her life fulfilled their dreams and prayers.
She mirrored that name too.
She looked upon each and every one of her family
As precious jewels.
A quality lady she was.
Judy Kay and Sally were, of course,
Her bejeweled daughters
Whom she treasured beyond measure.
Tommy John's stature as an outstanding man,
Even apart from his New York Yankees' star pitcher's classic role,
Fulfilled Opal's lifelong field of dreams.
Then, so very greatly,
The newer generation of charming grandchildren
Further enriched her days and ways.
Sounds of music encircled her heart
As her grandson Taylor's epochal career unfolded.
Future walks beyond the days
Of this life are now envisioned
Into and beyond the sunset of life;
Companionship with family lost is renewed
With God's rainbow in view.

Gladys

My Flower Lady,
Whose Love for Life I So Admired,
A Memorial Tribute.

Gladys was a quality lady
Who chose her friends carefully.
Her loyalty and respect for others were her hallmark.
Her days now will be spent in paradise.
Christ our Savior shows the way
For us to reach our reunions.
If Gladys were here today,
This is what I think she might say:
"A few days ago, I told my Jesus
That I was tired of my walker
And I wanted to come home.
I wanted to see my husband, James.
I wanted to see my sisters
And my mother, Mable.
I miss talking with my sister, Opal.
We were so close!"
Jesus said, "Gladys, throw away your walker
And stand tall and come with me.
I will give you a new body."
"How precious I feel being with family
And friends as I walk down the streets of pure gold."
Love comes from God out of heaven.
Let us treasure our pleasant memories
Of Gladys, who may be saying to us now,
"I want only happiness and cheer for you,
My loving family and precious friends.
May the best be left for last,
I leave you the love of my heart."

The Quiet Man

He was a quiet man.
He listened to learn.
He spoke to communicate worthily.
He selected his friends carefully.
He was loyal to his friends.
His marriage of well beyond half
A century spoke for itself.
Family came first, always.
Even the cat fared well by
His caring ways.
His interests included TV rodeos,
Antique bottle collecting, as well
As knives and guns.
His appreciation of life
Centered around Gladys, of course.
Even her apple pie and hot coffee
Meant so much to him.
All will agree that reunion
On the other side, by God's grace,
Is our prayer for Jimbo.

Holidays, Special Days, Any Day

Chapter Four

Attitude gets you thru a lot of life …

There once was a woman who woke up one morning, looked in the mirror, and noticed she had only three hairs on her head.

"Well," she said, "I think I'll braid my hair today."

So she did, and she had a wonderful day.

The next day she woke up, looked in the mirror, and saw that she had only two hairs on her head.

"Hmm," she said, "I think I'll part my hair down the middle today."

So she did, and she had a grand day.

The next day she woke up, looked in the mirror, and noticed that she had only one hair on her head.

"Well," she said, "today I'm going to wear my hair in a ponytail."

So she did, and she had a fun, fun day.

The next day she woke up, looked in the mirror, and noticed that there wasn't a single hair on her head.

"*Yeah!*" she exclaimed. "I don't have to fix my hair today!"

Attitude is everything. Have a good day!

Happy Valentine's Day

To the one I love,
I love the special time we share together;
Your precious warm kiss and your simple little hug
Last me until I hold you in my arms again.
I love the beautiful times when there is only you and I.
Just a simple touch of yours excites me,
Along with your lovely laugh and the secrets we share.
I can feel your thoughts and even your heartbeat.
I feel it any time you're in my presence.
My love, just to hold your hand
And know that you care is a godsend.
The thought of you brings a smile to my face.
Even when I'm sad I have no tears
For I know you are near.
You give me the strength,
Always, just for another day.
My dearest love, you are my all,
Forever and ever more.
When we first met, I knew from the start
I wanted you in my life.
And now each time I'm with you,
I know that to be true.
My darling, you are a part of my most intimate thoughts
When I retire for the evening.
I love all of you:
Your thoughts, dreams, and prayers.
You have a way of sharing yourself;
For this, my darling, I thank you.
You give me all of the wonderful possessions that I cherish.

Happy Mother's Day

You are that special mother these days.
The definition of family has changed so much.
Growing, making room for an even wider circle of love.
You will always be family, in closeness, caring, and love.
Being family isn't always easy,
But that is why family means so much—
To have children in your life.
You are that special mother who understands what love means.
Everyone's love is so important to you.
So, I wish you happiness on Mother's Day,
Because you make that difference in so many special ways.
I know I get sidetracked with all the things that happen in my life,
But my heart remembers how precious a mother is
Who listens to all the stories that children bring to the table.
My heart remembers how precious a mother's love can be.
My heart remembers every unselfish act,
Every piece of good advice a mother can give.
So now, it may seem I'm too old to remember all the things a mother
can do. So, I'll speak for your children when I say
Rest assured our hearts will never forget
That you are a great mother
And thank you for the thoughtful ways
You still show your love
And for the little things you still do
That make you that special mother.
Wishing you a day you'll remember.
For the special joys it holds
And the happy moments it brings to your heart.
Some things shouldn't wait for that special day in May.
Happy Mother's Day!

Thanksgiving

One of the busiest days of the year, Thanksgiving Day,
Yet the least talked about.
Every day that you wake up in good health should be a day of thanksgiving.
"Even a child is known by his doings, whether his work be pure, and whether it be right" (Proverbs 20:11).
So let us appreciate each day of our life,
For it is a day to be thankful.
We all drift in the steady stream of life
So quick (like a flash) our life will pass us by.
Our love is so soon forgotten,
So play hard and love long with your playmate while you can.
This alone is health and happiness.
If you believe this to be true,
You might want to follow this advice.
So soon night will fall
And leisure will be gone
And old age has counted the days,
As they have passed oh so fast.
We should cherish it all in our hearts.
Let us hold fast
All things that are beautiful while they last,
Beaten and tossed by sullen winds that blow.
My prayer, dear Lord:
Keep me eager; give me strength and courage to do my share; keep me aware to cultivate quietness and non-resistance, to seek truth and righteousness, to love, pray, and serve you cheerfully every day. May each soul be touched and blessed by this passage. When duty whispers low, God Almighty will know. Amen.

IF

If truly you care and passionately you seek
That all the credit and all the glory be totally His,
Then Our Heavenly Father will work wonders through you.
He will bring out the best of you each day.

Christmas

Real love is what I feel when I think of you.
You have given me so much good,
Never bad, never ugly.
You have given me all that is sweet, sincere, loving, and caring.
You are always there by my side to lift me if I stumble and fall.
I wait to share our daily triumphs,
Especially at Christmastime, when the weather is so brisk.
Christmas is a beautiful time of the year
Filled with laughter, love, and joy.
A special time to hold your hand,
And feel the warmth of your body by my side.
Your smile lights the room.
In your embrace, I melt away.
I've never loved anyone the way I love you,
And when we are together, I never want the time to end.
You are my dearest playmate,
My one and only true love.
I am so happy God brought you into my life.
I thank you for all the treasured moments you've given me,
And the rough times you've brought me through.
You warm my heart with your love and kindness,
My wonderful true companion.
How can I ever repay you for all the wonderful things you have given me?
Your warm love, true companionship, your precious time,
And most of all, the fullness of you.
Each day I am away from you
I miss your voice and the feel of your touch.
Today I thank you for making me a better person,
And I promise to love you the best way I know how.
You are my true playmate,
Best friend, the love of my life.

So Merry Christmas, my love, as we walk the pathway of life.

The one I can lean on,

Your tender heart comforts my soul.

All my favorite memories of us I've placed in a gift box wrapped with gold,

Tied with my heart strings and mailed …

To your heart for Christmas.

Anniversary
(Life, Freedom, and Happiness)

You've been a fantastic president,
Showing leadership, organizational skills,
And genuine friendship to all of us!
So tonight, as a special tribute to express our gratitude,
We wish for you an abundant life,
Full of freedom and happiness.
Now, to achieve this kind of fulfillment,
I offer, on behalf of our dance club,
Some pearls of wisdom
That have made my own life an incredible adventure.
Life truly is what you make it.
If you don't like it, change it!
In life you have a choice
To be free and to come and go as you wish,
With freedom to express your thoughts and feelings.
What are life and freedom all about?
Each of us strives for the ultimate goal: happiness.
Happiness, often elusive,
Comes to us in many different ways.
You can be happy on your job,
You can be happy with your mate;
But whatever you do in life,
It all comes down to having the right attitude
And having the love of God in your heart.
To be happy, you must live a simple life,
Be temperate in everything that you do,
And stay away from all self-seekers and all selfishness.
Let this simplicity be the top priority in your daily planning.
Think constructively,
And be accurate and crystal-clear in the decisions you make.

Cultivate a positive way of thinking,
Stay out of debt, and don't indulge in self-denial.
Always listen with an open and understanding mind.
Silence is what makes conversation real between friends.
Be grateful for your blessings
And for having the privilege of good health and even life, itself.
Let your thoughts be of peace and good will.
As you continue to prosper in life,
Give generously, letting divine inspiration be your guide.
Also, give love from your heart,
Asking for nothing in return.
Stay focused on keeping God number one in your life,
And He will do the same.
Keep your fears to yourself,
But share your courage with the world!
You need to concentrate on the immediate tasks at hand.
First, you must be happy in yourself
Or you will never experience complete fulfillment.
I think John F. Kennedy said it best:
"Happiness is the full use of your powers along the lines of excellence
And a life affording scope."
Your actions should be driven by your creed:
They take their hue from the complexion of your heart.
To be satisfied without having some of the things that you really want
Is a step forward in the pursuit of true happiness.
In short, we love you and will miss your smiling face.

For You and Les on Your Wedding Day

You are as good as goodness gets.
Just the thought of you
And the pleasant memories of you
Warm my heart.
Today is Les's and your day,
The beginning of a new journey
With two hearts beating as one.
You now begin an adventure
Of discovering your soul mate for life:
A friend, a partner,
The one you can love and talk to—
That special person
You will always need by your side;
One who can protect you and hold you
In the loneliness of a dark night
When there is a challenge
That you don't want to face alone.
Les can give you that strength and courage
To face any of life's problems
With true commitment, trust, honor, and love forever.
Yes, this is your day.
So live for the beauty of tomorrow!
May each day that follows
Be even better than the last,
Bringing you laughter, happiness, and sunshine
That will make your hearts sing.
The ceremony today reflects the love
The two of you share in this blessed relationship,
And may it grow deeper and stronger as the years go by.
Now, witnessed by friends and loved ones,
You have made a promise

That has touched the heart of our Heavenly Father.
Treasure your love,
Guard it with all your might,
And nurture and respect it
With a generous giving of yourselves to each other;
And you will have an abundant life that you both deserve.

Happy Fiftieth

With the memories of our hopes and dreams,
The adventures of a lifetime with a unique timeless tradition,
You have made the good times better.
You are that special person who I admire,
And you truly deserve your heart's desire.
You are the greatest spouse in the world.
You have made my memories sweeter,
My life brighter, and my love more real.
God has given us strength to raise our minds to higher daily expectations,
Giving each the knowledge to surrender our will with love to the other
And be as great as the dreams we choose to dream.
In the destiny we seek and the life God has blessed us with,
We think clearly, love sincerely, and trust each other without hesitation.
Let our honor, faith, and hope be our main sources of life
Till the dawn of eternity.
If we can aid someone in distress,
Making their burden less and spreading their happiness,
Maybe some other poor soul can rest.
I know if He can be by our side,
We change the lifeless wine of grief into a living goal,
With love that lasts forever that will make up life's completeness.
We are concerned with things as all are,
Facing the duty at hand with no regrets.
We care for the approval of our own consciousnesses
More than the applause of the crowd.
Today we celebrate fifty years of bliss—
Two people who have found love in each other through Christ.

Words to Think About While Dancing

A great use of life
Is to spend it on something that will outlast our own.
Life is like a pure flame
Heated by the sun during the day;
At nighttime, our hearts stand guard.
Be not afraid of life.
Believe life is worthwhile
And your faith will give you the answer.
The more a man knows,
The stronger he becomes.
The friendship of a great person
Is the favor of a greater person.
Keep your fears and your troubles to yourself,
But share your courage and happiness with all.
Let solitude reveal what we should be;
Not society dictating what we are.
Until I truly loved, I was alone.
Conversation enriches one's life,
But quietness is the beginning of learning.
Life can be more meaningful with a clear conscience
And trustworthy friends.
Great things are done when great people get together.
Weak men wait for opportunities;
Strong men make it happen.
When I hear it said that a young man could be a genius
I ask "What has he contributed to life?"
Remember, things don't happen
Until someone does something.
You will never know if the frog will jump
Until you touch it.

Legacy

I long to see the eyes of God.
I pray to work His plow and sing His song.
Then, from God's hand my life will be a legacy of love and faith.
By the grace of God, let me leave my footprint of commitment to the Lord,
I bestow the memory of what my father and his father have given me:
"Do unto others as you would have them do unto you."
My children will know that my faith has been steadfast
Because of the ministry and support of others.
Let me be remembered for my loyalty to God
And my commitment to family and friends.

About the Author

Joe Spears began his writing career during a stint as a company clerk in the army. At the age of twenty-two, he authored *How to Become a Millionaire* with only ten cents in his pocket. After rave reviews from friends and family, he wrote a second book, *Winning Laws of Life*. He then went on to write *Security, Success, and Happiness*, followed by *Invest in Yourself*.

In 1965, Joe graduated from Baptist Bible College in Indianapolis, Indiana. He entered the ministry and remained in Indiana as a minister for twenty-five years. Joe went on to become a successful contractor/builder, chef, tailor, and restaurant owner. Joe Spears became known as a modern-day Renaissance man. Throughout all of his career changes, Joe's love of writing never ceased.

Joe writes from his soul. Through the power of God's love and its translation in our daily lives, he shares his insight and words of wisdom. From the healing of the resentful heart to the healing of physical pain and mental anguish, Joe's writings illuminate the powers of God's light and love. He has written hundreds of love letters that have touched the hearts of friends and loved ones. He writes with a gentle, forgiving heart and is always endearing, insightful, and thankful in his observations.

Joe resides in Charlotte, North Carolina, and is surrounded by his loving family and friends.